THE MIDNIGHT CALLER

BY HORTON FOOTE

69589

━━━ A PLAY IN ONE ACT ━━━

DRAMATISTS
PLAY SERVICE
INC.

PRODUCED BY

SIDNEY BERNSTEIN

THE MIDNIGHT CALLER

by

HORTON FOOTE

DIRECTED BY: LEO PENN

CAST

ALMA JEAN JORDAN—*Age 38*	Mary James
"CUTIE" SPENCER—*Age 28*	Rebecca Dark
MISS ROWENA DOUGLAS—*Age 60*	Mary Perry
MRS. CRAWFORD—*Age 50*	Nora Dunfee
MR. RALPH JOHNSTON—*Age 35*	Justin Reed
HELEN CREWS—*Age 28*	Patricia Frye
HARVEY WEEMS—*Age 30*	Robert Morris

Harrison, Texas

PRODUCTION DESIGNED BY: BOYD DUMROSE

STAGE MANAGER: GENE JONES

MUSIC BY: FRED HELLERMAN

Opened July 2, 1958
Sheridan Square Playhouse

3

THE MIDNIGHT CALLER

The living room, part of the front yard and part of a small bedroom of Mrs. Crawford's boarding house in Harrison, Texas. The living room occupies most of the stage area. It is mainly defined by the use of furniture but there is a very low wall down L. to suggest a bay window, a screen L. C., for masking an entrance, an open arch D. R. to indicate the front door, and stairs U. R. leading to bedrooms. An entrance above stairs, U. R., leading to dining room. The living-room is furnished with a small sofa, with a low table in front, R. of C., a small chair up C., a hassock, a low table and a rocking chair near the suggested bay window. Directly up stage is a raised platform large enough to have a small bed and a table with a lamp. This becomes the bedroom of Helen Crews. This area is only lit when used in the action. The section of the yard visible is immediately in front of the front door of the house, extending across down stage to the corner of the bay window.

Alma Jean is seated on small armchair, working a crossword puzzle. Cutie enters through arch D. R.

CUTIE. Hey, Alma Jean.

ALMA JEAN. Hey, Cutie. You're late.

CUTIE. I know, I had a hard day. I had so much work to do and I decided to stay until I got everything finished up.

ALMA JEAN. You're a fool. I'm here to tell you that you're the biggest fool in the whole state of Texas. Mr. H. T. Mavis works you until it's a shame. Do you think he appreciates it? No, indeed. Why you got fifteen dollars less bonus than I did last Christmas.

CUTIE. I like the work.

ALMA JEAN. You're a fool. Well, I don't know. Maybe we're all fools. What kind of a life is this, living in this one-horse town, pounding typewriters all day? (*Miss Rowena Douglas comes into the room, up stage L. Miss Rowena is in her sixties. She has a pleasant, sweet face. She dresses a bit eccentrically, and rather dramatically. Right now she has on a very feminine tea gown.*)

MISS ROWENA. Dear ones, forgive me for comin' to supper this way, but I have to dress for tonight and I just thought I'd take my bath before supper and put on somethin' rather informal. Dear Mrs. Crawford tells me this is my last opportunity to dress so informally with the gentleman comin' tomorrow to live in our midst. It'll be excitin', won't it, girls, havin' a real, live man amongst us. A mature, distinguished man from all I've heard.

ALMA JEAN. They're all the same if you ask me. Personally, I think Mrs. Crawford is makin' a mistake not holdin' out a while longer until she can have a girl here. I won't feel comfortable with a man in the house. I can tell you that.

MISS ROWENA. You won't feel comfortable? Why not, honey?

ALMA JEAN. I just won't. I have to work with them all day at the court house. I don't want to have to live in the same house with them.

MISS ROWENA. Now, Alma Jean, don't be bitter. It doesn't become you. . . .

ALMA JEAN. I'm not bitter. I just don't like a man runnin' around the house I live in. If I had, I would have gotten married a long time ago.

CUTIE. Did Mrs. Crawford tell you she'd rented the other room, too?

MISS ROWENA. Another man, honey?

CUTIE. No, ma'am. Helen Crews and her mama have had a falling out over Harvey Weems and she's movin' in here.

MISS ROWENA. Well, I declare.

ALMA JEAN. (*Stopping her work at the puzzle.*) Cutie Spencer, you don't mean what you're sayin'?

CUTIE. Oh, yes, I mean it. Of course, I mean it.

ALMA JEAN. Has Mrs. Crawford lost her poor mind? You don't mean to tell me she's invited Helen Crews to live here.

CUTIE. I didn't say she invited her. I reckon Helen came and asked her for a room . . .

ALMA JEAN. That settles it. I'm movin' out. I'll live in a tourist court before I'll put up with that.

CUTIE. Now what is the matter with you, Alma Jean?

6

ALMA JEAN. (*Rising.*) What's the matter with me? I don't want my reputation destroyed utterly. I cherish my reputation. I have watched all my life that no one can hold up one spot of blemish against my reputation.

CUTIE. And how in the world is this going to affect your reputation . . .

ALMA JEAN. Helen Crews' name is on the tongue of everybody in Harrison and you know that as well as I do. Her own mama has ordered her out of her house . . .

CUTIE. Well, what if she has?

ALMA JEAN. What if she has . . .

CUTIE. I think her mama is half crazy. And she's mean as she can be. All I can see that Helen Crews did was fall in love with the wrong man.

ALMA JEAN. Oh, is that so?

CUTIE. Yes, ma'am, that's so. And you know as well as I do that if they had gotten married like they planned the whole thing would be forgotten . . .

ALMA JEAN. Not by me. I can tell you that. Never by me.

CUTIE. How can you be so hard, Alma Jean? How in the world can you be so hard? . . .

ALMA JEAN. I am not hard.

CUTIE. You certainly are.

ALMA JEAN. I am not and I won't have you say I am.

CUTIE. Well, I think you're being very hard . . .

ALMA JEAN. Well. And I don't intend to stay here and be insulted. (*She marches out of the room. She goes up the stairs, up stage* R. *The crossword puzzle is left on table.*)

CUTIE. Oh, my goodness.

MISS ROWENA. You'll have to beg her pardon, Cutie, the poor girl can't help behavin' like that.

CUTIE. I will not beg her pardon. I spend half my life begging her pardon. I will not . . .

MISS ROWENA. Yes, you will, honey. Yes, you will. (*Miss Rowena crosses to rocking chair, down* L.)

CUTIE. I know. I guess I will. (*She goes to the stairs. She starts to call. Then she thinks better of it.*) Well, I'll wait for a while. Harvey did love Helen Crews, Miss Rowena, I don't care what anybody says.

MISS ROWENA. (*Sitting in chair.*) I believe it.

7

CUTIE. Why, I was goin' with Skeet Williams at the time. And they were best friends from boyhood. And Skeet told me that Harvey Weems told him many a time that he loved Helen. And look what she did for him. (*Cutie crosses to hassock. She sits.*)

MISS ROWENA. I know it.

CUTIE. Why, Harvey used to slip out of his mama's house every night of his life before he started goin' with Helen and get dead dog drunk and ride all over Harrison County until he'd just pass out.

MISS ROWENA. I believe it.

CUTIE. He told Skeet all about it. He said after he met Helen he'd call her up any time of the day or night and she'd get in the car with him and ride until his nerves were calmed. He said one night they rode to the Gulf and he asked Helen to marry him and she said she would if he swore never to touch another drop of whisky and right then and there he took his whisky bottle and threw it in the Gulf and it just floated away and for the longest kind of time he never took another drink.

MISS ROWENA. I believe it. I believe it. And probably never would have had another drink if they had gotten married. And I bet they would have been married if his mama had stayed out of it and her mama had stayed out of it.

CUTIE. Well, they didn't. And they'll never get married now. I knew that when he left town with his mama and stayed away those six months. And now he's back and drinking and Helen won't see him. And I don't reckon I blame her.

MISS ROWENA. Isn't it a shame? Harvey Weems was the handsomest boy I think I ever laid eyes on, don't you, Cutie?

CUTIE. Yes, ma'am. I think without a doubt he was.

MISS ROWENA. And rich. Had everything in this world, it seems like, to make him happy. . . . (*Alma Jean comes into the room from stairs.*)

ALMA JEAN. If you care to apologize, Cutie, I'll come back in the living room.

CUTIE. All right. I'll apologize, Alma Jean.

ALMA JEAN. O.K. I accept the apology. (*Alma Jean crosses into room.*) But I'm not hard and I'm not bitter and I don't appreciate you and Miss Rowena saying so.

CUTIE. Well, you may not be hard and bitter, but you're too sensitive for your own good and that's the living truth.

ALMA JEAN, I'm not sensitive

CUTIE. You are.

ALMA JEAN. I'm not.

CUTIE. O.K. Let's change the subject. You're not. (*Cutie crosses to sofa.*)

ALMA JEAN. Do you think I'm sensitive, Miss Rowena? (*She goes over to Miss Rowena.*)

MISS ROWENA. Do you want the truth, honey?

CUTIE. Yes.

MISS ROWENA. All right. I do. I'm not blamin' you for it, but I do. You can't be sensitive and endure our life, honey. You'll be torn to pieces if you continue to be. . . .

ALMA JEAN. What's wrong with our life? I like my life.

MISS ROWENA. Do you, Alma Jean?

ALMA JEAN. Yes I do. Don't you?

MISS ROWENA. No. I don't like mine. I could think of a million other lives I'd rather lead, if I let myself, but this is my life so I try and make the best of it. (*Alma Jean looks at her like she thinks she's crazy. Miss Rowena goes to the window and looks out.*) I love the fall. I love the smell of the wood smoke. I love the coolness in the air and I love the look of the skies at night. The stars seem so much brighter and closer.

ALMA JEAN. I think the fall is real dull unless you like football and I can't stand football. Everybody tryin' to hurt everybody else.

MISS ROWENA. I always feel a little lonely in the fall though. Everything seems to me a little lonely; the stars and the sky and the trees. Wonder why that is?

CUTIE. Hadn't thought about it.

MISS ROWENA. I said good-bye to Robert Henry in the fall and to Chester Taylor. . . . I never said good-bye to Lee Edwards. My mama insisted I stay in my room and she said good-bye to him. (*Pause.*) I love Friday nights though. Winter, spring, fall. . . . Life always seems so carefree and frivolous on a Friday night. Don't you love Friday nights, Cutie?

CUTIE. Yes, ma'am. I do.

MISS ROWENA. Ever since I was a little girl I've looked forward to Friday nights. It was always the night I felt free of responsibilities.

9

ALMA JEAN. I'd like them better if I had Saturdays off like you do.

MISS ROWENA. Well, that's why teachin' school is the loveliest job there is. You're always sure of bein' free on Saturday and Sunday. (*A pause. Miss Rowena continues standing at the window.*)

ALMA JEAN. Miss Rowena, what are you doin'?

MISS ROWENA. Watchin' the lightnin' bugs. They'll be gone before we know it. Now that summer's over. (*Mrs. Crawford comes into the room from the dining room entrance up* R., *followed by a man. Mrs. Crawford is an energetic woman of fifty or fifty-five. The man is the new boarder, Ralph Johnston. He is in his middle thirties, nice looking, neatly but inexpensively dressed.*)

MRS. CRAWFORD. Girls, I would like you to meet our new guest. He arrived a day early. . . . (*The three women rise.*)

MISS ROWENA. Oh, heavens, Mrs. Crawford, I'm so embarrassed, look at me.

MRS. CRAWFORD. You look all right to me.

MISS ROWENA. But I'm not dressed to meet a gentleman.

MRS. CRAWFORD. You look fine to me. Now, Mr. Johnston is just gonna be treated like homefolks like everybody else. . . . (*Mrs. Crawford points to Miss Rowena.*) This is Miss Rowena Douglas actin' so coy over here, Mr. Johnston.

MISS ROWENA. Mr. Johnston.

MR. JOHNSTON. How do you do.

MRS. CRAWFORD. And Miss Cutie Spencer.

CUTIE. Hey, there.

MRS. CRAWFORD. And Miss Alma Jean Jordan.

MR. JOHNSTON. How do you do.

MRS. CRAWFORD. Like I told you girls, Mr. Johnston moved here from Teague. He's to be with the Gas Company.

MISS ROWENA. How lovely. I hope you'll be happy here, Mr. Johnston.

MR. JOHNSTON. Thank you. (*He goes to a chair.*)

MISS ROWENA. I bet you don't know what I'm doin' here at the window screen, Mr. Johnston.

MR. JOHNSTON. No, ma'am.

MISS ROWENA. Tell him, Alma Jean.

ALMA JEAN. Watchin' lightnin' bugs.

MISS ROWENA. What do you think of that, Mr. Johnston? I'd

10

like a penny for every hour I've spent at the window or the screen door watchin' lightnin' bugs. It's a custom I've brought with me from my childhood. I was a lonely child, Mr. Johnston, because of my frail health, and to amuse myself at the twilight I used to sit at the window or the screen door by the hour and watch and count the lightnin' bugs.

MR. JOHNSTON. Is that so? (*A woman's voice calls from outside* D. R.: "*Mrs. Crawford.*" *Mrs. Crawford gets up from her seat.*)

MRS. CRAWFORD. Come on in, Helen. (*Helen Crews comes in the front door, down* R. *She is a mature-looking girl in her late twenties. She has a strong face, with a great deal of sensitivity about it. She is carrying a suitcase.*) Put your suitcase by the stairs, Helen, and come say hello to everybody. (*Helen puts her suitcase by the stairs and comes into the room.*) I believe you know everybody, Helen, except Mr. Johnston. This is Miss Crews, Mr. Johnston. She's coming to live here too.

MR. JOHNSTON. How do you do, Miss Crews.

HELEN. How do you do.

MISS ROWENA. Welcome, Helen.

HELEN. Thank you.

CUTIE. Hello, Helen.

HELEN. Hello, Cutie. Alma Jean.

ALMA JEAN. How do you do. (*She gets up and walks up the stairs.*)

MRS. CRAWFORD. Come on, Helen. I'll show you to your room.

HELEN. Thank you. (*They go out, up the stairs. Helen takes her suitcase. Miss Rowena is looking out the window.*)

MISS ROWENA. There's goin' to be a full moon before the night's over, Mr. Johnston. A harvest moon. I think the harvest moon is the most romantic of all. The saddest and the most romantic. Spring's way behind and the summer's in the process of being forgotten and the winter won't be long in comin'. (*A pause. She laughs.*) But I guess just the old people think of things like that. The young people don't. They laugh and chatter all day in school just the same, winter, spring or fall. (*Mrs. Crawford and Helen come back in from stairs.*)

MRS. CRAWFORD. Let's all go in and eat. Where's Alma Jean?

CUTIE. You all go ahead. I'll call her. (*They all go into the dining room. Cutie goes to the door and calls: "Alma Jean. Supper." She stands at the stairs waiting. Alma Jean comes in.*) Alma Jean,

I think that was the rudest thing I ever saw. I wouldn't treat another human being that way no matter what in the world . . .

ALMA JEAN. You tend to your own business. I'll act just as I please. I'm not payin' my good money here to get lessons in manners, Miss Cutie Spencer. You be polite to those you want to be polite to and I'll be polite to those I want to be polite to. (*Mrs. Crawford comes in from the dining room.*)

MRS. CRAWFORD. Come on, girls. Supper's on the table.

CUTIE. Yes, ma'am. (*They both start for the dining room. The lights dim, and come up on Helen Crews' room on up stage platform. It's later that night. Helen has been busy putting her things away. There is a knock on her door.*)

HELEN. Yes? (*A man's voice calls out: "It's Ralph Johnston."*) Just a minute. (*She quickly puts a few scattered personal things away and then opens the door.*)

MR. JOHNSTON. Been unpacking?

HELEN. Yes, I have.

MR. JOHNSTON. So have I. All through?

HELEN. Just about.

MR. JOHNSTON. Would you care to ride down town with me and have a drink?

HELEN. Oh, no, thank you. I'm very tired.

MR. JOHNSTON. Oh. Well, I suppose it is kind of late.

HELEN. Another time.

MR. JOHNSTON. Sure. Do you work in Harrison, too?

HELEN. Yes, I do. I'm a stenographer.

MR. JOHNSTON. Oh. Were you born around here?

HELEN. Yes, I was born here in Harrison.

MR. JOHNSTON. Oh. Well, good night.

HELEN. Good night. (*He goes. She closes the door. She switches out the light from behind the door. She falls across the bed crying. She sobs for a moment. There is a knock again at the door. Very gentle this time and hesitant. She quickly dries her eyes. She calls:*) Yes?

MR. JOHNSTON. (*Calling.*) It's Ralph Johnston again. Is everything all right?

HELEN. Yes. Everything is all right. Thank you.

MR. JOHNSTON. O.K. (*He goes on. She hears him go down the stairs. She turns the lights back on. She starts to unpack again, when she starts again to cry. This time silently. She sinks into a* chair, covering her face with her hands. *The lights dim and come up on the living room of the Crawford house. Cutie comes in, finds a magazine and starts to read. Miss Rowena comes in the front door.)*

CUTIE. How was the bridge party?

MISS ROWENA. Fine. There were just two tables. What did you do?

CUTIE. Went to the picture show. *(Miss Rowena sits in the cane rocking chair.)*

MISS ROWENA. Everybody else in bed?

CUTIE. Looks like it. I don't really know. I just got here myself, lights were all out upstairs. I asked Alma Jean to go to the picture show with me, but she said she wasn't speakin' to me and shut her door in my face.

MISS ROWENA. Well, I know you'd like to get married and I want you to get married, but I hope for all our sakes that Mr. Johnston takes a shine to Alma Jean and marries her. I think we'd all be so much better off. Don't you?

CUTIE. *(Giggles.)* Yes, ma'am. *(A pause.)* I'm never going to get married, Miss Rowena.

MISS ROWENA. Now don't say that. Why would you say that? A nice pretty girl like you.

CUTIE. I say it, because I know it. I'll never be asked now. Oh, I'm not bitter about it, mind you. It would have been nice, but I know it'll never happen. I'll be workin' for Mr. Mavis and livin' at Mrs. Crawford's until I'm ready to go wherever lady stenographers go to.

MISS ROWENA. Don't talk foolish. *(A pause.)* I'll see you get married yet. I'll see you get married and Helen and maybe even Alma Jean. *(She looks at the window.)* Look, Cutie, yonder it comes over the tops of the trees. Yonder comes the harvest moon. *(Cutie comes to look at the window. Alma Jean and Ralph Johnston come in the front door D. R.)*

ALMA JEAN. Hello, Miss Rowena. Hello, Cutie.

MISS ROWENA. Hello.

CUTIE. Heh.

ALMA JEAN. I've been showin' Mr. Johnston the sights of Harrison. I was sittin' here all alone and feelin' awfully sorry for myself, when Mr. Johnston asked me to ride to the drugstore for a drink.

13

MISS ROWENA. Won't you sit down, Mr. Johnston?

MR. JOHNSTON. Thank you, ma'am, but I think I'll go on up-stairs. I'm real tired. (*He starts for the stairs.*) Thank you, Alma Jean, for coming with me.

ALMA JEAN. That's all right. I enjoyed myself.

MR. JOHNSTON. Good night, you all. (*The ladies all bid him good night and he goes up the stairs. Alma Jean looks to see if he's gone. She goes over to the others.*)

ALMA JEAN. I found out a lot about him. His wife and he just got a divorce. I think he's very lonely. He asked me all about you all. I told him a thing or two.

CUTIE. I bet you did.

ALMA JEAN. Now what do you mean by that remark?

CUTIE. Nothin'. Now don't be sensitive, Alma Jean.

ALMA JEAN. He said he thought he heard Helen cryin' in her room. He asked me if she had any troubles. I said plenty. I put him straight about her right away. He seemed very surprised.

MISS ROWENA. Oh, I saw poor Harvey Weems walkin' around the square drunk as I was comin' home. It was the first time I'd seen him since he came back from his trip. It gave me such a funny feelin'.

ALMA JEAN. Well, I hope he don't come around here hollerin' for her. I'm puttin' my foot down if he does. (*Helen comes down the stairs.*)

HELEN. Oh, I didn't know anyone was in here. I couldn't sleep.

CUTIE. Pull up a chair and join the sorority. We were just dis-cussin' our new male roomer.

HELEN. Thank you. (*She sits on the sofa. Miss Rowena gives an-other little gasp of excitement.*)

MISS ROWENA. Just look at the moon, girls. Just look at that full moon. (*She looks up at the sky.*)

> "I see the moon
> And the moon sees me,
> God Bless the Moon
> And God Bless me."

(*She looks at the other women.*) Look at the moon, girls. Look at the harvest moon. (*The four women look at the moon. The lights fade. They are brought up again. It is two weeks later on a Friday night. Miss Rowena, Cutie and Alma Jean are in the living room.*

14

Miss Rowena is in the rocker. Cutie is on the couch. Alma Jean walks around the room.)

ALMA JEAN. Well, Miss Crews and Mr. Johnston are out together again. I don't understand it. He knows perfectly well what kind she is. Well, that's a man for you. I'm not surprised his wife divorced him. *(A pause.)* Well, I'm a nervous wreck. I don't know about you all. I told Mrs. Crawford today that if something wasn't done about the situation I was definitely goin' to have to look for another place. *(A pause.)* Look there. There it starts. There goes a car drivin' slow. They're expectin' a show.

CUTIE. Alma Jean. I swannee you have the biggest imagination.

ALMA JEAN. It's not my imagination. It's all over town that four nights last week Harvey Weems came over here at twelve o'clock and stood out in the front yard and cried and called Helen's name. Of course that didn't bother her. She has no shame. She walks down the streets of the town just like nothin' has happened.

MISS ROWENA. Honey, she is mortified by it. She told Mrs. Crawford so when Mrs. Crawford spoke to her about it.

ALMA JEAN. Then why doesn't she do something about it?

CUTIE. Alma Jean. What can she do?

ALMA JEAN. She can tell him to stop.

MISS ROWENA. But I'm sure she has, honey. He only comes around when he's drunk. She can't help that. What else can she do but have him arrested and you know none of us want to see poor Harvey arrested.

ALMA JEAN. All right. Take up for her. But if it happens again either I go or she goes and I told Mrs. Crawford that. And if she stays Mrs. Crawford will only be able to get riff-raff in my place. No self-respectin' person will move in here with her under the same roof. And I told Mrs. Crawford that.

CUTIE. Let's change the subject.

ALMA JEAN. Why?

CUTIE. Because I'm tired of talkin' about it. There are other things in the world to talk about.

ALMA JEAN. Not as far as I'm concerned. This is the burning issue as far as I'm concerned. *(She goes to the door u. r. and calls:)* Mrs. Crawford. Mrs. Crawford. Come out here, if you please. There's another car goin' by slow. It's the third one in the last half-hour and don't tell me it's my imagination. This house is becomin' a place of curiosity just like her mama's house used to

15

be. Pretty soon they'll be chargin' admission to hear her midnight caller cryin' in the front yard and callin' her name. (*A pause.*) What has she got? Will you tell me what has she got? I understand the appeal of Gene Tierney or Rita Hayworth. But Helen Crews? She's a perfectly plain girl.

CUTIE. Helen was always quite popular with boys, Alma Jean.

ALMA JEAN. With what boys? Drunks and divorcees? Yonder comes the fourth. The fourth car in half an hour. (*She runs to the stairs calling.*) Mrs. Crawford. Mrs. Crawford. (*Mrs. Crawford calls back: "I'm coming. I'm coming."*) I feel like a freak in a side show.

MISS ROWENA. Well, honey, those cars are not comin' to see you.

ALMA JEAN. Yes. But they're comin' to see the house I live in. (*Mrs. Crawford comes down the stairs.*)

MRS. CRAWFORD. Now what is it? I was in bed asleep.

ALMA JEAN. In bed asleep. Well, I wish I could sleep. I haven't closed my eyes for a week. The fourth car just passed by here driving slow and gaping.

MRS. CRAWFORD. How do you know?

ALMA JEAN. How do I know? I know. Because I heard people up town today sayin' they were gonna be out tonight for the show. Because everybody in town knows how he comes into our yard and carries on. Because her own mama told me today it was the same at her house, every time he started drinking. Only in those days Miss Helen used to go out to him and get in a car and drive off with him at twelve or one or two o'clock in the mornin'. That's the kind of a girl she is. That's the way she and her mother had their fights. That poor mother. . . . She knows what kind of a girl Helen Crews is. . . . (*Helen has come in the front door.*)

HELEN. You don't know what you're talkin' about, Alma Jean. You don't know at all what you're talkin' about. (*Alma Jean starts up the stairs.*) Did you hear what I said, Alma Jean? You don't know what you're talkin' about.

ALMA JEAN. There's nothin' I have to say to you.

HELEN. There's plenty I have to say to you.

ALMA JEAN. Well, I don't intend to listen to it. (*She starts for the stairs. Helen grabs her by the arm.*)

HELEN. You will listen to it. You will listen to every word of it. Just what did my mother say to you? (*A pause. Alma Jean doesn't*

16

answer. She turns and looks at Helen defiantly.) Did my mother say that she never wanted me to go with any boys? Or my sister? Did she tell you that my sister ran off to get married and my mother has never spoken to her since? Did she tell you that? Did my mother tell you that I never left the house in my life on a date without a fight? Without such a fight that the whole evening was ruined for me? Did she tell you that?

ALMA JEAN. I don't know anything about that. . . . I . . .

HELEN. Of course you don't. Well, there's lots you don't know. Did she tell you that I loved Harvey and that Harvey loved me and that we were going to be married . . .

ALMA JEAN. Well, if you love him so much how can you go runnin' off every night with the first man that asks you for a date?

HELEN. I said I loved him. And I did love him. I loved him for four years. I stood by him for four years. And don't forget that I stood by him in spite of his mama and my mama, and I fought to win him. And I almost won but I didn't win after four years, so I quit. Because I had to quit. Because I've seen too many people spend their lives fighting fights they can't win.

MISS ROWENA. Girls! Let's don't get on with this, we're all excited. Here comes Mr. Johnston. Now, let's just change the subject.

MRS. CRAWFORD. Alma Jean is just a little high-strung, Helen. She doesn't mean a thing she says. She really has the best heart in the world. She just hasn't had much rest lately because of Harvey's visits . . .

MISS ROWENA. Sh. Now let's all just change the subject. Let's all talk of pleasant things. Here comes Mr. Johnston. (*Ralph Johnston comes in the front door.*) Hello, Mr. Johnston. Come, pull up a chair.

MR. JOHNSTON. Thank you. (*He sits in the small armchair. There is an uncomfortable silence.*) I wish I could find a garage a little closer for my car at nights, Mrs. Crawford. It's a little inconvenient walkin' two blocks in rainy weather.

MRS. CRAWFORD. Well, I'll inquire around and see if I can't locate a place for you. (*There is another uncomfortable pause.*)

MISS ROWENA. Look at the leaves fallin'. The leaves are fallin' so fast. Pretty soon the pecan trees will have no leaves at all. How's the pecan crop gonna be, Mrs. Crawford?

MRS. CRAWFORD. I think it's gonna be all right. First norther they'll come falling onto the ground. Then I'm gonna rout you all out of bed to help me pick them up before they get stolen away. I think it's awful the way people will come into your yard and help themselves to your pecans. Don't you?

ROWENA. I do. I thnk it's perfectly awful. (*Cutie suddenly starts to cry.*)

CUTIE. Excuse me. I'm sorry. (*She goes running up the stairs.*)

MISS ROWENA. Poor Cutie. I think it's awful the way she has to work. That job is makin' her nervous. Don't you think so, Mrs. Crawford?

MRS. CRAWFORD. I guess so. (*There is another uncomfortable silence. Alma Jean goes up the stairs.*)

MISS ROWENA. My goodness, everybody is so high strung tonight.

MRS. CRAWFORD. Well, I think we'd all better get some sleep.

MISS ROWENA. I think so. (*She starts out.*)

MRS. CRAWFORD. Good night.

MISS ROWENA. 'Night. (*They go up the stairs. Ralph Johnston goes over to Helen. He tries to take her in his arms and to kiss her. She moves nervously away from him.*)

HELEN. I'm sorry, Ralph. I'm sorry. . . . I guess I'm nervous tonight like everybody else because of my midnight caller. (*A pause.*) I think I'd just better give up the ghost and move away. It'll make it easier certainly for Harvey to do whatever he has to do, and my mother and his mother and me.

RALPH. Helen . . .

HELEN. Harvey can't go or wouldn't if he could. And what do I do? How can I stop a gentleman who's had too much to drink from coming to my front yard at night and callin' my name? Ask him? I have. Beg him? I have. (*She looks up at the sky.*) The leaves are fallin'. Falling all over town. The streets will soon be covered and the yards. (*A pause.*) Oh, it all began so long ago that I don't remember the beginning and so how can I possibly know the end? And I don't know who to blame. My mother? For wantin' to keep me and my sister locked up with her forever? How can I blame her? We're all she had. My father died when we were just babies. We were literally all she had. (*A pause.*) My mother never liked Harrison. She wasn't born here, she was born fourteen miles out in the country on a farm. Maybe she should have stayed there. Maybe it would have all been different. . . .

18

She was very rich at one time. My father lost everything speculating on the cotton market. Maybe my father's to blame. Or Harvey's mother. . . . Or Harvey. Or me. I've spent many an hour trying to figure that one out and I can't figure that one out. (*A pause.*) Of course, I don't regret it. You understand that? I don't regret it at all. He was lonely and I was lonely and he needed me very much at the time and I needed him. Of all the people in the world then, you would suspect of being lonely, Harvey Weems was the last. And yet for all his beauty and his good looks and his money, he was the loneliest person alive. He was lonelier than I was and that was very lonely. I remember the day I discovered that. I came into the drugstore and he was sitting at the counter and we spoke, and though I'd known him all my life, I looked at him this day as he spoke and I knew then how lonely he was in spite of his looks and his money. And I guess he knew I knew. And I guess he wanted to be saved from his loneliness and I wanted to be saved from mine, because two days later he called and asked me for a date. And those nights, then, he came to my window and called to me it wasn't for lack of respect like people think. It was because Mama would answer the phone without my knowin' and not tell me he had called. She hated him from the first in spite of his money and his good looks and his family name, just like his mama hated me from the first. And their hate licked us, because what was the need to end our loneliness turned into a battle between four people and then the town. (*We hear a man's voice down the street calling Helen's name.*) Yonder he goes. Like some lost ghost calling my name. He's so drunk, he's forgotten where I live. (*A pause. She cries out.*) I tried to save him. I wanted to save him like I never wanted to do anything in my life. But I couldn't win. I reckon I didn't know enough. But if I had known enough, how could I have won? How can you save someone that doesn't want to be saved? Because he doesn't want to be saved. Not from drink, not from loneliness, not from death. And you have to want to be. And that's what I've learned from these four years. (*Harvey Weems has come into the yard from the R. He stands very quietly, singing softly to himself. He is very drunk. There is a kind of dignity in his drunkenness. Helen sees him. She goes quickly to him, out the front door, calling softly as she goes.*) Harvey. (*He doesn't answer if he hears or sees her. He stands there immobile singing quietly to himself.*) Harvey . . . (*Harvey doesn't look up. He stands with his head down singing:*)

HARVEY. "Blessed be the tie that binds . . . In Christian Brotherhood . . ." (*Harvey starts to cry. It is a quiet kind of crying, pathetic and moving. She goes to him. She touches his arm in warmth and compassion.*)

HELEN. Don't cry, Harvey. Please don't cry. I can't stand to see you cry. You go home now. (*Harvey looks at her for the first time.*)

HARVEY. Helen . . .

HELEN. Harvey, please go home. I worry about you when you're out alone this way.

HARVEY. Come with me, Helen. I'll get my car and we'll ride and ride and ride . . .

HELEN. We've been all through that, Harvey. I can't go with you.

HARVEY. Please, Helen.

HELEN. I can't. (*Harvey looks at her as if he heard her for the first time.*)

HARVEY. You can't ride with me, Helen?

HELEN. No.

HARVEY. Who's to ride with me, Helen?

HELEN. I don't know.

HARVEY. (*He is crying again now.*) I'm lonely. I'm so lonely.

HELEN. Please, Harvey. (*Harvey controls himself. He looks at her.*)

HARVEY. Are you mad at me because I'm drinking?

HELEN. I'm not mad at you.

HARVEY. But you don't love me any more? (*Pause. She doesn't answer.*) Do you love me any more?

HELEN. No, Harvey.

HARVEY. Why, Helen?

HELEN. I just don't, Harvey. You go home now. (*He stands as if he hadn't heard her. He quietly begins his song again.*)

HARVEY. "Blessed be the tie that binds . . ." (*Mrs. Crawford and Miss Rowena come into the living room from stairs. Cutie and Alma Jean are behind them. They look out the window and the front door. Mrs. Crawford goes out to Helen in yard.*)

MRS. CRAWFORD. Helen, please get him to go home.

HELEN. I'm tryin', Mrs. Crawford, I'm tryin'. . . .

ALMA JEAN. (*At window.*) Look yonder. Yonder goes a car.

20

Drivin' slow. (*She screams.*) Move on. There are decent people livin' here.

MISS ROWENA. Sh, Alma Jean.

ALMA JEAN. Puttin' on a side show at twelve-thirty in the morning. Somebody call the Sheriff.

MISS ROWENA. Sh, Alma Jean.

ALMA JEAN. He's crazy. You ought to lock up crazy people. (*Helen has Harvey by the arm again.*)

HELEN. Please, go home, Harvey.

HARVEY. You want me to go home?

HELEN. Yes.

HARVEY. Then I'll go home. (*He starts out. He pauses.*) Good night, Helen. Pleasant dreams, Helen.

HELEN. Good night, Harvey. (*He starts slowly out of the yard. He goes out* R. *Helen stands watching him go. Mrs. Crawford goes back into house. Miss Rowena comes outside. She stands close to Helen.*)

MISS ROWENA. He's drunk. He's so drunk. Where's it gonna end, Helen? Where's it gonna end? I taught Harvey, you know. I was teachin' music appreciation in those days. I remember I had the fifth grade and I taught Harvey to sing, "When Day Is Done." He sang it beautifully, too. Sang it before the whole school assembly, as I remember. Oh, he's so drunk, Helen. Where's it gonna end? Where's it all gonna end?

HELEN. I don't know, Miss Rowena. I don't know. (*Miss Rowena goes back into the house. Mrs. Crawford turns to Cutie and Alma Jean.*)

MRS. CRAWFORD. All right, girls. Let's all get some sleep now. (*She takes them by the arm and they all go up the stairs. Helen is still standing there. Ralph Johnston comes over to her.*)

HELEN. (*Turns to Ralph and embraces him.*) Help me, Ralph. Help me. Help me. Help me. (*He holds her in his arms for a moment. She sobs. He is holding her closely, passionately. The lights fade. The lights are brought up on the living room of the Crawford boarding house. Miss Rowena is there. Cutie comes hurrying in. It is late the next afternoon.*)

CUTIE. Miss Rowena. Miss Rowena . . .

MISS ROWENA. What is it, honey?

CUTIE. Alma Jean is in her room packing.

MISS ROWENA. What?

21

CUTIE. She's in her room packin'. She vows her mind's made up. She vows she's leavin' us.

MISS ROWENA. Oh, now she mustn't be hasty. I'll go talk to her right away. (*Mrs. Crawford comes in from the dining room.*)

CUTIE. Mrs. Crawford. Do you know that Alma Jean is upstairs in her room packing to leave?

MRS. CRAWFORD. Why, no.

CUTIE. She is. I talked to her for half an hour tryin' to change her mind. She says that nothin' can change her mind after last night. . . .

MRS. CRAWFORD. That silly girl.

CUTIE. She says she can't go on livin' here. She says that Harvey Weems comin' here every night is makin' her very nervous. She said she made nothin' but mistakes today at her work. She says . . . (*She cries.*) It's makin' me nervous, too. I'm sorry I don't like givin' way to my feelin's this way but something has to be done. It's makin' me extremely nervous, Mrs. Crawford. I made mistakes all day today, and I couldn't eat lunch and I have a splittin' headache . . .

MISS ROWENA. I know. I know just how you feel, Cutie. You needn't apologize. This can't go on, they'll have to lock the poor boy up . . .

MRS. CRAWFORD. They have. I just talked to the Sheriff. They locked him up late this afternoon.

MISS ROWENA. They have?

MRS. CRAWFORD. Yes, ma'am. It was at the request of his mother. (*A pause.*) After he left here last night, he tried to harm himself.

CUTIE. Oh, no.

MISS ROWENA. Harvey Weems?

MRS. CRAWFORD. Yes, ma'am. He tried to hang himself.

MISS ROWENA. Harvey Weems? The handsome Harvey Weems? Oh, I'm sorry. I'm so sorry. I'm so sorry. (*A pause.*) I taught him in school, you know. It doesn't seem like more than yesterday I was teachin' him in school. I had him in music appreciation and I taught him to sing, "When Day Is Done." He had a sweet voice. A lovely, sweet voice. And now they've locked him up. (*Alma Jean comes down the stairs into the room.*)

ALMA JEAN. Mrs. Crawford, I suppose you've been informed by Cutie of my decision. I've given you plenty of warning, you'll

22

have to admit. I told you over and over that I was reachin' the breakin' point . . . (*She looks at the women.*) What's the matter? What's happened?

CUTIE. They've locked up Harvey Weems. He tried to harm himself.

ALMA JEAN. Oh, I'm very sorry to hear that. When did that happen?

CUTIE. After he left here last night.

MRS. CRAWFORD. The Sheriff just called me. I had left a message for him to call. I felt I had to put in a complaint after what had been goin' on here at night. I didn't want to, you understand, but I felt I had to. . . .

CUTIE. Of course you did.

MRS. CRAWFORD. Well, anyway, I did. And he said it was all right, now, because they had locked him up.

ALMA JEAN. Is that so?

CUTIE. So now you can unpack, Alma Jean.

ALMA JEAN. Oh, no, thank you. I'm goin' anyway. This house has changed with that divorced man here and that woman. I don't care to stay any longer in this house.

MRS. CRAWFORD. Well, suit yourself about that, Alma Jean, but they're leavin' too.

ALMA JEAN. Leavin'? Where are they goin'?

MRS. CRAWFORD. They're goin' to Houston. They're gonna be married.

ALMA JEAN. Oh.

MRS. CRAWFORD. Helen called me from work to tell me. They're leavin' tonight.

MISS ROWENA. That's lovely. Isn't that lovely? (*Cutie starts to cry.*)

CUTIE. What's the matter with me? I cry over the least thing these days. I cry when I hear Harvey Weems is locked up and I cry when I hear Helen Crews is gettin' married.

ALMA JEAN. Well, in that case, I'll stay. I'll unpack my things. (*Helen and Mr. Johnston come in from outside. Alma Jean leaves the room. Miss Rowena goes up to them.*)

MISS ROWENA. We heard the news, honey. We just heard the news and we're rejoicin' for you.

HELEN. Thank you.

MISS ROWENA. I think you have the loveliest and the sweetest bride in Harrison, Mr. Johnston.

MR. JOHNSTON. Thank you, ma'am.

MISS ROWENA. And to think it happened here, Mrs. Crawford! Romance bloomed and blossomed here in this very house.

MRS. CRAWFORD. I know.

CUTIE. Congratulations to you both. (*Again she starts to cry.*) Excuse me. (*She goes up the stairs.*)

MISS ROWENA. Poor Cutie has been very emotional lately. . . .

MRS. CRAWFORD. Helen, will you all be here for supper?

HELEN. No, thank you, Mrs. Crawford. We have our packin' to do and we don't want to get in to Houston too late. I'll leave our address with you before we leave in case anyone wants to get in touch with us.

MRS. CRAWFORD. All right, Helen.

HELEN. We'll say good-bye before we leave.

MRS. CRAWFORD. All right, Helen. (*Helen and Mr. Johnston start towards the stairs.*) Helen . . . (*Helen stops.*)

HELEN. Yes?

MRS. CRAWFORD. Helen . . . did you hear . . .

HELEN. About Harvey?

MRS. CRAWFORD. Yes?

HELEN. Yes, ma'am. I did. I had to go and talk to him before he'd go. (*She cries.*) Oh, it was awful, Mrs. Crawford. It was just awful.

MRS. CRAWFORD. I'm sorry, Helen, to have brought it up. I just thought if you didn't know . . .

HELEN. I know. (*She turns to Ralph.*) Come on, honey. (*They go up the stairs.*)

MRS. CRAWFORD. I'll get supper on the table.

MISS ROWENA. Yes, ma'am. (*Cutie comes back in the room. She picks up the crossword puzzle. The lights dim and come up on Helen's bedroom. Ralph knocks.*)

HELEN. Come in. (*Ralph enters the room.*)

RALPH. All ready?

HELEN. Yes, I am. Are you?

RALPH. Uh . . . huh.

HELEN. Ralph.

RALPH. Uh . . . huh?

HELEN. Maybe I should wait a few days . . .

24

RALPH. What for, Helen?

HELEN. Maybe there's somethin' I can do . . .

RALPH. There's nothin' more you can do. You were told that.

HELEN. I know.

RALPH. You waited four years, Helen.

HELEN. I know.

RALPH. Come on, Helen. You're to be my wife now. Come on.

HELEN. All right, honey. (*He kisses her and holds her close. Then he picks up the suitcase once more and they go out, closing the door. The lights dim and come up on the living room. Mrs. Crawford sits on the couch, reading. Cutie sits on the hassock. Miss Rowena is in her rocking chair.*)

MISS ROWENA. Wonder what's playin' at the picture show? (*No one hears her.*) I said I wonder what's playin' at the picture show?

CUTIE. A Western at one and a gangster at another.

MISS ROWENA. Oh. (*Helen and Ralph come into the room from upstairs.*)

HELEN. We're all ready. (*Mrs. Crawford gets up.*)

MRS. CRAWFORD. Well, we're gonna miss you two.

HELEN. Thank you. Good-bye, Miss Rowena. Good-bye, Cutie. (*Miss Rowena and Cutie and Mrs. Crawford hover about them. They wish them good-bye. Congratulations, etc. Ralph and Helen start out.*) Tell Alma Jean good-bye for us.

MRS. CRAWFORD. I will. (*They leave, going out front door. Miss Rowena looks out the window after them. She waves good-bye once more.*)

MISS ROWENA. There they go. There they go. (*She turns back from the window. Mrs. Crawford goes to the stairs and calls:*)

MRS. CRAWFORD. Alma Jean. You can come down now. They're gone. (*Mrs. Crawford goes to sofa, sits.*)

CUTIE. It suddenly seems so quiet and so still. It's no quieter than usual, I suppose, but it seems that way. I reckon we were all so on edge half waiting to hear Harvey every night, that we were gettin' sensitive to the least noise. I know I was. (*Alma Jean comes down the stairs.*)

ALMA JEAN. Thank goodness things are back to normal for a change. (*A pause.*) Oh, well, I hope you've learned, Mrs. Crawford. Men and women don't mix. There's bound to be trouble when men move into the same house with women. I've been livin' in boardin' houses for seventeen years and I never saw it to fail, once a man moves in trouble begins. I could have had him, you know. If I'd wanted him. He asked me out that first night, you remember. But I let him know that I had my mind on other things. Besides I didn't think he was one bit attractive, did you?

MISS ROWENA. Yes, I did, honey. I must admit I thought he was very attractive. (*Cutie starts to cry again. She gets up and goes out the front door.*) Poor thing. She's been cryin' at the least provocation. (*She goes to the rocking chair by the window.*)

ALMA JEAN. Well, they can call me an old maid if they want to. But I like my peace and my quiet.

MRS. CRAWFORD. I guess we all do, Alma Jean. (*Alma Jean goes over to the crossword puzzle at the table. She picks it up.*)

ALMA JEAN. I've seen the girls that get married. I wouldn't trade places with a one of them. Not one. I can go where I please, do what I please, spend my money like I please. (*She takes the crossword puzzle and goes to a chair.*) Every friend I have that's married envies me. (*Mrs. Crawford is dozing on the sofa.*) It would take more than Mr. Ralph Johnston to make me give up my independence. I went with a boy once in high school. I almost married him, too. Then my mother took me aside and gave me a good talkin' to. She let me know how hard she had to work. She said she had to work harder takin' care of children and a house than five women at the court house. The next night when my friend came to call I wasn't home. (*She sees Mrs. Crawford is asleep and not listening. She puts the crossword puzzle down. She goes over to Miss Rowena.*) I bet everybody sleeps good tonight.

MISS ROWENA. I think a good norther would help us all. It's too hot for this time of the year. We are way in November.

ALMA JEAN. I know it. Well, that's the trouble with this part of the country. You either freeze to death or you're burnin' up. Never any moderation. (*Cutie comes in the front door.*)

MISS ROWENA. Lights are goin' on all over town. I love to see the lights go on.

CUTIE. Yes, ma'am.

ALMA JEAN. Anybody care to have a little game of honeymoon bridge?

MISS ROWENA. I don't believe so, thank you.

ALMA JEAN. Cutie?

CUTIE. No, thank you.

26

ALMA JEAN. I tried workin' the crossword puzzle tonight. Did you?
CUTIE. Uh, huh.
ALMA JEAN. That was the hardest crossword puzzle. I see no reason in makin' them so hard, you can't work them. Do you?
CUTIE. Nope. (*Alma Jean looks over at Miss Rowena.*)
ALMA JEAN. What are you doin', Miss Rowena? Countin' lightnin' bugs? . . .
MISS ROWENA. No, ma'am. Just thinkin'.
ALMA JEAN. What were you thinkin' about?
MISS ROWENA. Thinkin' about how it was quiet and not quiet. Thinkin' about how one person ends up in the crazy house and thinkin' how another goes off to get married. And others sit on front galleries and rock their lives away. Thinkin' about all the things I've seen an' heard sittin' on the front galleries of Harrison. Thinkin' about how I'll never sit on this gallery again, without hearin' Harvey Weems as he walked drunk through the streets of the town callin' the name of Helen Crews. . . . Thinkin' about . . . (*Away off and very far in the distance we hear Harvey calling, "Helen. Helen."*)
CUTIE. You hear him?
ALMA JEAN. He's callin' from the jail.
MISS ROWENA. So he is. (*We hear the call again.*)
CUTIE. You hear him? (*We hear again: "Helen. Helen."*)
MISS ROWENA. She's gone, Harvey. Gone to Houston. Gone . . . (*She has whispered this so he couldn't possibly have heard her, but the town is silent once more except for the rocking of Miss Rowena's chair.*)

CURTAIN

PROPERTY PLOT

Crossword puzzle, pencil—Alma Jean
Suitcase with clothes in it—Helen
Magazines on one of the tables in living room

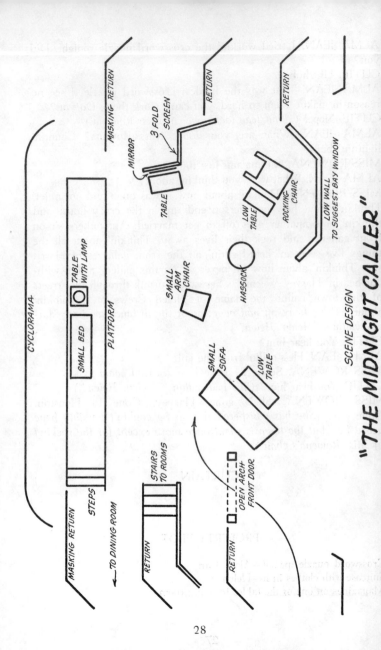

"THE MIDNIGHT CALLER"

SCENE DESIGN

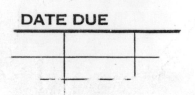

DATE DUE